The Linnet's Wings

THREE POUNDS OF CELLS

Three Pounds of Cells

by

Oonah V Joslin

Copyright Notice

Ordering Information:
Single Copies available from our website:
www.thelinnetswings.org
Quantity sales. Special discounts are available on quantity purchases by corporations, associations, and others. For details, mail the publisher at the address above.

ISBN: 978-0-9930493-7-8

Editor: Kathleen Cassen Mickelson

Layout and Design: Marie Fitzpatrick for "The Linnet's Wings"

OFFICES

Online: Zoetrope Virtual Studio,

The Linnet´s Wings Submission Office

Surface:

Design, Carchuna, Granada, Spain

Publishing, Mullingar, Co. Westmeath, ROI

Other Publications by The Linnet´s Wings

Classic: "The Song of Hiawatha" by Henry Wadsworth Longfellow ISBN 13: 978-1480176423

Classic: "The House that Jack Built" by Randolph Caldecott, ISBN-13: 978-1483977669

"One Day Tells Its Tale to Another" by Nonnie Augustine ISBN-13: 978-1480186354

"About the Weather-- Spring Trending" by Marie Lynam Fitzpatrick ISBN-13: 978-0993049330

"This Crazy Urge to Live" by Bobby Steve Baker ISBN-13: 978-0993049-0-9

"A Christmas Canzonet" (Classic and Contemporary Poets, and Classic Art) ISBN-13: 978-1522710714

"Disabled Monsters" by John C. Mannone ISBN: 13: 1522869504

Acknowledgments

I gratefully acknowledge the following venues that first published versions of these poems.

Bewildering Stories ("Fenestration," "Rhythm of Rain," "My Aspen at Wallington," "To Prometheus Bound," "Tapping the Salamander," "The Long Wave," "Ludek's Dawn," "Ships," "The Smith's Gold," "Change Has Tenses All Its Own," "Winter's Last Breath," "Stain of Light," "Voluntary Exile," "Art of the Storm," "Music to my Ears," "Touching the Tiger")

Blink Ink ("Dream of a Frost Sprite")

Gyroscope Review ("Minneapolis' Natural Jazz," "Heart of Brightness," "Pipestone," "A Cemetery Just Around the Corner")

Ink Sweat & Tears ("The Rain")

Ofi Press ("Phase Transition")

Postcard Poems & Prose ("Purple")

The Linnet's Wings ("Advent")

The Pygmy Giant ("On An Old Carousel")

The Shine Journal ("From Crazy Diamond to Borrowed Light," "Tryst")

My heartfelt gratitude goes to:

My sister Esmé who has been since childhood my most valued critic.

Marie Fitzpatrick, Editor of The Linnet's Wings, who suggested I put together this collection.

Kathleen Cassen Mickelson, Editor of Gyroscope Review and my former co-editor at Every Day Poets, for using her considerable skills in editing this work and for her friendship and encouragement throughout.

James Graham for his constant and generous comments over the past decade at Writewords. (www.writewords.org.uk) and for his advice on aspects of this book.

Pippa Little, Geraldine Green and John Stocks for reviewing Three Pounds of Cells and giving me confidence to forge ahead.

Don Webb and John Stocks (Bewildering Stories) and Dave Morehouse (Postcard Poems & Prose), who have collectively published more of my work than any other editors.

Last but not least, I remember my Writewords friends John Duncan Ritchie, (d.Nov 2014) and Robin Herrnfeld, (d.July 2013) who have gone ahead to light the way.

Dedication:

I dedicate this to my patient teachers, loved ones and
mentors and to all who have inspired me, those beings
brave and curious enough to wonder where the light
and music come from.

Table of Contents

PHOTOGRAPHY

Introduction

"Once I knew only darkness and stillness…my life was without past or future… but a little word from the fingers of another fell into my hand that clutched at emptiness, and my heart leaped to the rapture of living." Helen Keller

Our perceptions and interactions make us uniquely who we are. The moment we become aware, everything speaks to us – not only people but animals, objects, music and art. Poetry first spoke to me because I was a slow reader. Poetry was short. I could manage a poem in reading time at school, going over and over it. Rhymes and rhythms helped me overcome my difficulties. "The Cat and The Moon" by Yeats was one of my first loves. I inhabited that poem and it made me want to write poems too. It spoke of love, fear and hope, and of imagination. It showed how much of our own natures is locked up inside us – far more than we understand.

How little we understand of ourselves. The brain is a great mystery. No use waiting 'til it's dead and dissecting it. We can scan it live, but we will not find the mind. The mind is an emergent property that is constantly changing, mapping our past and influencing our future. Just as the mind is an emergent property of the brain, might there be an emergent property of humanity? An emergent property of the universe? Might that property not be Being itself? Consciousness? And might that Consciousness be God?

We live in this marvellous universe of matter, light and energy exchanges. We perceive light and sound but it is our minds that create art and music, language and poetry. What is it that makes humans spark with creativity? What is this need to make ourselves heard within the vastness? Where do we come from and where are we going?

This collection of poems explores some of the things that have spoken uniquely to me in my life, people, places and art that have inspired me – not least the ever-changing sea. Light and music are my very first memories; disjointed, non-verbal memories encapsulated in 'Parameters of Perambulator.' But memories are selective, individual, inaccurate and I have the poorest memory. So what's really real? Dreams aren't real are they – or do all our experiences contribute to personal reality – even our nightmares? The human brain – three pounds of cells – is how we make sense of the world but I have always wanted to believe that we are parts of an emergent property, bigger than our limited perceptions. And when those perceptions are no more, I don't want to be consigned to dark silence. Scatter my ashes on the sea so I can sparkle and roar a while more.

FOREWORD
(For Oonah)

It is an honor when a colleague asks you to read their work and comment on it. It is especially an honor when you know this person is talented, when their way with words makes you a little bit jealous.

Reading Oonah's poems for 'Three Pounds of Cells' reminded me of the scope of her vision. In these poems, she lays out her evolution as a poet who recognizes the smallness of our species in the far greater universe. Her poems examine these brains of ours that let us experience the richness that surrounds us, hear the symphonies both natural and man-made, see the colors and feel the pulse of life.

I've known Oonah for quite a while. We were on staff together for five years at the online poetry journal 'Every Day Poets,' which published from 2008-2014. We went back and forth on other poets' work, negotiated all kinds of revisions, and faced off over rejections and acceptances. We pooled our talents to make ourselves and the poets we published proud.

That's not an easy task. But working together in this way made us both better editors and better writers.

Oonah came to visit me in Minnesota once, along with her husband Noel. I took them to Pipestone National Monument, where Native Americans have quarried the red pipestone to make prayer pipes for generations. During our walk around the quarry area, Oonah sat down in front of a rock formation known as Birdman and waved Noel and me away so she could be alone with her thoughts. I was pleased to see those thoughts come to fruition in the poem

"Pipestone":

Red burn the prairies where
their blood seeped to the seam:
close beneath the quarry path

I see
by rock am seen.

Poets let themselves be taught and, in return, offer their interpretations to us all. Watching Oonah take in Pipestone, seeing her synthesize an ancient sacred message from a culture not her own, struck me as a lesson in how humanity is more than the sum of its parts. That came back to me as I read through these poems, saw the way the baby in the perambulator reached out to the world and never stopped. Three Pounds of Cells moves from that first awareness we all get to have, to all that there is, with room to contemplate what lies between.

- Kathleen Cassen Mickelson
April, 2016

Manhattan Skyline Nov 2013 – Oonah V Joslin

Section One

Parameters of a Perambulator

action

light

action

touch

feel

me

not me   me   not me
something other   something farther
near   far
near far touch
feel toes
me
toes   hands
me
string of toys
not me

light action cry

face smile

dappled   light   on

ceiling far beyond me

light programme   music far

beyond me

entire world far
beyond

me

in my pram

Fenestration

Vindauga — Wind eye.

Admitting more than light and air
inviting the eye to wander here and there
wonder at nature's visions
ponder on acts of saints
covet goods in gaudy display.

Eagbryl — Eye-hole.

Inside, outside,
no longer speaks of
dark and light
as it used to.

Skins, paper, lead, horn, glass,
photons;
innovation
breached all barriers to
today.

These words would not exist
in a world without
windows.

From Crazy Diamond to Borrowed Light

Facetious I may be at times
but you have light
enough and light to spare
and share,
and see me shine.

The light is yours,
only the surface mine.

You focus; illuminate.
I scatter and reflect.

I may accumulate in time
wisdom to kindle,
like the star you are.
But unless a light be brought to it,
even a diamond cannot dazzle.

Manhattan Rain Has Farther To Fall

From the entrance to the mall
every shape and shade of tall
assaults my small-town eye,
pins me to the pavement,
draws me skyward.

A suicide of shafts
shard Seventh Avenue.
A million bits
drill down,
curtain windows
floor by floor
and drown in city roar.

It washes my memory so
I can recall no rain
gentle on field, hedge-height
or falling grey on grey
from sky to shore
before this rain
ran through me.

Manhattan rain has farther to fall:
the threat and thrill of it.

Minneapolis' Natural Jazz

Science of sound café
suspended scales

forty five feet from
the ceiling of the atrium
one hundred and fifty
resonating tubes
pick up the signals
amplify the sound
played on marimba,
xylophone, wooden jugs,
rhythms and styles, faster tempos, more voices
suited to the size and location of
the Quake.

This is the music of the seismofone
ladders that link our thoughts deep into Earth.
As we eat we are reminded by
occasional, random, strangely calming notes,
the crust beneath us is
in constant motion.

The Rain

When the rain began, people rushed out to gather as much as they could. It was real. All denominations. Money.

Wealth beyond avarice.

Then came the day it changed. It burst into flames and scorched their eager fingers, sticking like napalm. They ran for shelter into buildings that caught fire, into churches, into their cars. They fled the city; took refuge where they could.

They sought the high ground.

At Angel Hill crowds gathered having abandoned their vehicles. There it was safe, but vast violent storm clouds veered across the valley and away down to the west, lowering, ever closer; menacing. Each separate soul watched in awe, awaiting whatever would drop from those clouds.

I waited too.

The rearing front legs of a white steed emerged, and the rider, too bright to behold, silver gilt, thundered into being. Many perished at the sight of him. His companion followed close on a chestnut battle stallion, striking red sparks on the earth, cleaving heads with a fiery sword.

As he passed he bent and breathed to me.

'I have not come for thee.'

From the blackest of the clouds and blacker still rode Want, and emaciated all whom he had governed. I saw their papery shadows, two dimensional, cast to the wind like worthless promissory notes. In his wake the pale rider descended. His horse, grey, tinted with all the phosphorous corruption of decay.

He had his rights. I was bone.

I tried to remember hope.

Unreality Realised

The knife
    The blade
        The threat of violence
            lucid

My intervention
pushed roughly aside.

The knife
    The blade
        The threat of violence

On the landing
the ugly scene
me in between.

Back to bed with me
and tuck-me-in
and calm me down
and comfort me again.

Forget it now
    Forget it
        Now
It is forgot
by everyone but me.
Persistent in my memory
decades later I recall

The knife
        The blade
                The threat

That never happened, Dear, they say.
It was a nightmare.
You were always such a sensitive child,
remember.
        Remember?
                All I remembered was
The knife
        The blade
                The threat

Rhythm of Rain

this morning's music
a pitter of rain on glass

plip into the bird bath
plok against a bucket in the yard

drum on nylon stretched out over spokes
swish of wet rubber on road

at the door I hold out my hand
feel the silent wetness of the sound

Heart of Brightness

Never imagined it would be like this:
like a diamond.

A jewel from the air
casting light in all directions,
scattering the sun
like so much tinsel.

A jewel on the ground,
sharp and facetious,
cut to impress.
Its movement Cartier precise,
intricate, perpetual.

Soon your own heart keeps
that relentless beat.
Your feet pick up the pace.
Your mind accepts the clamorous roar
as waves crashing on a rocky shore,
a restless storm in a vast forest,
animal bellows, shrills and shrieks,
siren calls.

Down in the street in the dizzy deep
of lacerating power, you meet
hard edged faces, inward looking,
sharp and quick as knives.

Many have been cut down here:
crushed, pulverised, buried alive
and dead.
It demands reflection,
worship.
No excuses.

But when you expect it least
it reins in to a trot,
lies still as schist,
invites you to
'Imagine'
an open glade; allow
the ghosts of time to invade
your circle of its sky.
Buildings hedge you round
like sentinels.
Nurtured and anonymous;
you're almost safe.

And after dark, there is no darkness here.
The diamond lights itself internally.

Dreams and shadows put on a show.
You walk a broad way
among mortal stars so close
you might almost think them real.
Diamonds are facetious.
They are carbon like all of us.

See the place
where black dust fell:
a reverberating avalanche
at the stone heart of her
flaws.
A canker at the Apple's core.

Consumed.
Consummated.
Never imagined you would love her so.

Section 1
Appendix

Fenestration: Old Norse; 'vindauga', from 'vindr – wind' and 'auga – eye'
Old English; 'eagþyrl', literally means 'eye-hole.'
Window 13th century; originally referred to an unglazed hole in a roof.
In English the word fenester was used as a parallel until the mid-18th century and
fenestration is still used to describe the arrangement of windows within a façade. Also,
words such as "defenestration" are still in use today.

From Crazy Diamond to Borrowed Light: For John Duncan Ritchie valued friend and
mentor. D 2014

Minneapolis' Natural Jazz: "An instrument inventor hears music everywhere." Trimpin
– who designed the seismophone at the Science Museum of Minnesota.

Heart of Brightness: To my astonishment, I fell in love with New York. The Imagine
mosaic in Central Park is in memory of songwriter John Lennon.

Cafesjian's Carousel at Como Park, St. Paul, MN – Oonah V Joslin

Section Two

My Aspen at Wallington

My aspen quakes at the least breath of air
and makes a sound like heavy rain as I
sit in the shade, listening to its soothing
song of life-giving droplets, remembered.

In autumn it recalls what made it grow
so tall and sturdy and with leaves so broad.
It digs deep to summon from Spring the zing
of refreshment and the pale blue sky. I

thought it didn't know it was my aspen
but when I touch its bark it quivers so,
surrounds me with familiar pitter-pats
of sound. And, as I walk away, a breeze
gently draws across its boughs. A duet
composed by wind and tree plays just for me.

The Brynmill Bird

Down by the pond an insistent 'Hello.'
'Hello' I said before wondering
who the speaker was.
'Hello Hello.'
A big black Mynah.
'Oh what a pretty boy!' I said.
'Bugger the ducks,' came the reply.
'You're so clever,' says I.
'Bugger the ducks.'
And some blue haired lady would look
askance. After all, there were children around.
I got him to say it every time I had a chance.
He taught a toddler or two.

You couldn't call it a conversation. More
a performance. He'd versed me in my lines.
'Hello, Mr Mynah. Where's the ducks?'
'Bugger the ducks! Bugger the ducks!'

I liked him.
He knew his mind.
He was forthright and vociferous;
consistent, if not kind
and he knew a thing or two
about ducks in general
and blue haired old biddies.

South Wales Echo

Mary's voice was audible above the city traffic noise.
She was a constant.
many layered,
a bag, a shopping arcade, a history.

I was all high hopes with half a bed-sit.

Her atonal notes,
expressed the urban opera;
a dissonance within the crowd.
Stout hand weathered with grime
permanently cupped for change,
she never begged.

I never gave.

One day I offered her a meal
in a café.
She looked at me aghast,
shuffled away.
I drew my smug conclusions
as her diva voice
faded between the shops:
one single, long, passionate outpouring.

When Mary died
'The South Wales Echo' carried the news.
A voice was silenced in the Land of Song.

I hear her still sometimes
shrill down the years.

To Prometheus Bound

Years since, I heard dark canvas calling,
a skeletal ghost, mouth wide in silent scream,
head thrown back, eyes closed,
shoulders hunched, fingers cringed in pain.
Fragile figure.
Broken frame.

Is that a cloak
or tattered wing you wear?

How your head droops now down and away;
transmuted agony,
exhausted resignation,
a long exhalation of despair.

What elusive colours made you?
Nothing in art is ever black and white.

I see a slit of light;
a window there to your right
casting a pool of hope upon the floor.
I interpret the spirit of a door;
steps leading up through you.

You have not yet been painted long
my friend. Does it seem eternity?

I spoke in kindness yet you turn in anger.
Gone in an instant. You pity human kind.

Wear penance Whitby-black. Your
undying fingers grip the rock.
You are a prayer stretched thin. Bone,
kneeling in the dark,
humbled by hope,
brought to your knees by love.

We are kin longer than this decade past
and that first day you called to me.
I thought I'd discovered all at last;
yet just now you reached out towards
that box.

Can you lock it? Do you hold the key?
Well, I will forgive you, if you will forgive me.

Pipestone

Quarter mile distant
crumpled edge
rose quartzite quarry
sacred red
waters took them
down Winnewissa falls.

Red burn the prairies where
their blood seeped to the seam;
close beneath the quarry path
I see
by rock am seen.

The Great Spirit illuminates
bids me contemplate.

We share the rock face
to face never again to be
Birdman and me
as we are now
unchanged.

Quartzite covered ancient bones became pipe stone,
Oracle of many suns and sons' stories,
sages, springs, red clays, sumac fires.
iyansha K'api; that is to say,
'the place where one digs the red rock'
to carve the calumet
make its stem of prairie wood

                              honour all that grows
leather and feather
                              honour all that lives
make smoke rise to the skies
                              honour the earth
with simple tools and sweat

let no weapon be brought upon it
let no blood be shed.
Take only what I teach you from this place
of peace and shadows' change.

Shadows change.
Birdman gone. The world awaits.
Blood of nations, sacred seam within,
I go.

Even rocks crumble so.

Oonah V Joslin

Tapping the Salamander

The salamander will no longer breathe
fire, suck oxygen, make the air a fume
of stinking vapours wound around the town.

They will bleed the blast to its hearth;
leave cold the grim grey nugget of the beast
accursed yet beloved, slag at its heart.

See the steel tongue curl and writhe with flame,
loll in a last exhalation of liquid heat.
Death throes on the floor of industry.

28
The Linnet's Wings

On An Old Carousel

Pretty painted horses going nowhere
preserve the illusion;
fun of the fair
embalmed.

Not a mechanical failure,
this stasis. One feels
the music might start up at any moment
the march continue, the tango
tango on, the Wurlitzer waltz
whirl. Heads thrown back whinnying,
alive with gold and turquoise,
silver shod, grey-maned, red-throated
life
proudly presents the B flat chord — ta-daa!
Silent
the shellac book of notes is
still.

The last ride's done.
A simple stepping off.

"There is no wealth but life." John Ruskin

Almost on Brantwood Jetty

Old Man Coniston fishing the lake
catches and casts October light
a-lap-lap-lap and a Wild Cat Cruise
the poot-poot of the bright steam yacht
her serpent prow gleaming gold against sage
ripples a million scales of sound and shade

and a child bird-free from the school-yard
lap-lap-laps up life life life, singing a singsong
looser than loose, looser than looser than loose loose loose
he sings to his runkled self in the water,
answers to birds and his artless self and no one else
exists and life is all his wealth.

Woo-hoo! The boat takes up the cry. The boat,
a ghost once swallowed by the lake, makes
mountain ridges echo its cloudy breath, beats
an arm, a fist, a fiery breast. A nest of petrified peaks
hold up the bluebird sky in elemental rituals.
On the margins, I alone am tenuous.

Better Than Half

For my husband Noel

Sometimes the past is blank as the future.
Like when you talk about one day in May
years ago and in some place I swear I've
never been. That woman in the hotel
corridor, that man in the street who looked
just like, and might in fact have been, someone
I'm sure I've never heard of. You restore
minutiae of my history, colour
my days like a magic paint book, affirm
what we laid down. And I am safe as long
as you remember me in all the times
and places of our life. It frightens me
to think were I alone, how very blank,
how incomplete, my single self would be.

Section 2
Appendix

My Aspen at Wallington: Wallington House and gardens is located about 12 miles west of Morpeth, Northumberland, England. It was donated to the National Trust by Sir Charles Trevelyan in 1942, complete with estate and farms – the first donation of its kind.

The Brynmill Bird: Brynmill Park is in Swansea, Wales.

South Wales Echo: The South Wales Echo is a daily newspaper in Wales.

To Prometheus Bound: an ekphrastic poem after the oil on canvas painting of that title by Yorkshire artist Robert Ford. "Whitby-black" refers to the town's long trade in the finest jet jewellery and also to the fact that I encountered the painting there.

Pipestone: After a visit to Pipestone National Monument, Minnesota.

Tapping the Salmander: A salamander refers to all liquid and solidified materials in the hearth of a blast furnace below the tap hole. The salamander includes liquid iron and slag and mixtures of solid iron, slag and coke/carbon.

On an Old Carousel: Cafesjian's Carousel is housed in Como Park Zoo and Conservatory, St Paul Minnesota. It is over 100 years old and still in working order.

Almost on Brantwood Jetty: Brantwood was the Lake District home (Cumbria, England) of John Ruskin, writer, geologist, botanist, philanthropist, political reformer and patron of the arts. An extract of this poem appears on a National Trust postcard – the first to advertise the Steam Yacht Gondola that works Coniston Water.

Prince Regent Inlet, beyond Bellot Strait in Canadian Arctic, Wojtech Jacobson

Section Three

Tryst

At the turn of the tide
in an off shore wind
the beach rushed to the sea.
With a silver tinkle,
wind whipped, shifting shingle
swept across wet sands,
obliterating
the time that lay between.

Phantasmagoric fingers formed and fanned,
keen to caress
the wave's white spray,
tossed back
in a delight
of intimacy,
unzipping blue,
unzipping green,

'Come taste my salt again.'

The Long Wave

I love the long wave's brown and breaking curve,
a billion bubbles percussive, shimmering;
how the power of tide incoming
shatters shells, leaving silence shivering on the air.

The sea seems angry sometimes in the wind;
sage-grey waves on blustery days
whip my breath away,
diminished to the horizon.

Shipping passes. Turbines turn.
Cormorants dry their wings,
angel-poised on any solid thing.
Gulls swirl and gannets thunderbolt
into the steely squall.

But most I love the brown-blue silk shimmer
of offshore vanilla ripples,
that seam of indigo stitching sky and sea
nebulous, where everything agrees to be divided.

Ludek's Dawn

Standing amid a symmetry of sky and sea
rippling like the destiny
of the sail that drove him

towards mackerel sky and mackerel sun
burning the horizon.
Like a latter day Moses

standing there with God
no mountain now, no desert, no
commandment on His lips

only the gifts
of sea and sight
and silence.

Ships

You lifted a concept from the shadows
on a drawing board, flat and unpolished;
paper, sand-paper, stranded, sanded wood;
modeled it, toyed with it. You called it 'she,'
shared in her longing for a ceaseless sea.

'A mast is not a mast that has no sail,'
you heard her wail.
'A sail is but a canvas without wind,'
her paint complained.

Unbound her from her ropes, you set her free
to dance in her own elemental way
breathing an ecstasy of storm and sky
wave after wave of crystal-splintered light
from dawn to sinking sun daring the day,
far, far from the idea she once was,
far from the sea-bed skeleton she'll be.

Holy Island Haibun

In a café out of the rain that hadn't let up all afternoon,
restless children and parents moan, "We're never coming
here again. There's nowt to do."
Thunder brattles embattled clouds like ships of heaven run
aground. On sandbanks seals cry like disembodied souls.
Lightning illuminates the ruined priory and sheep sheltered
in the lee of castle walls.
The tide turns and the malcontents escape over the
causeway to Northumberland: across that stretch of
understanding that separates those who bring their solace
with them and those who'll never find it anywhere.
Up on the Heugh we await the baptism of fire that blazes
from beneath low, purple cloud in the clear aftermath of
evening sky.

No holy theme park
here but sea, light, air. Listen.
Seals cry Cuthbert's tears.

A Song of Seals

In gold spooned moonlight
banked against purple cloud
sanded seals sing
evensong;

a-low
hallo-la-loo
a halle-lu-ja-
weh halloo-la-loo

sing songs of shipwrecks, sirens, saints and plunderers
along the wave lengths of legend,
shadowed in Long Stone light.

They sing the priory's arch in echoed sound
built high to span
the stranded causeway
isle to land;
to span centuries.

Lights to port and starboard blink red, green;
speak to an unseen hurry of shipping
silently slipping past.

Lights ashore carry coffee-sipping colonies splitting through fields;
an orange streak on metal rails into the darkness passes
past the past and on and on
to the mournful cry

hoo-hoo-la-loo

echoes,
left behind
unseen, unheard, unhindered,
a cross
on sacred banks.

As I Remember It

Here I learned
the secrets of life.
How solid things
are eaten away
like rock,
rotten teeth,
sweet friendship;
how time makes everything
grainy.

A smell of steam coal as we approached
the buffers. The clickety-clack
replaced by laughing wind,
a screech of screams from the big dipper,
the sticky avalanche of penny falls,
the transitory nature
of ice-cream and sunshine.
Sunset bats off-shore
take to the sky.
Skerries.

It was a coast that rattled and rumbled;
ghost trains basalt-black
and giant dreams a-crumbling.

Here's the harbour where
the wave of youth crashed over
me clinging to any rock until I found

one so solid it clung back
anchored to love's soft lies.

Purple

a deeper blue
pumps through the red veined sky
a better brown
curls round the roots of land
reflections and diffractions fill the sea
marooned on the edge of day
a feeling I rise or set by

Heart of Stone

Lithophone
made in stone
quarried, assembled, sounds
like a million water-mallets'
piston strokes falling lightly
not to choke its ringing tones.

Sound waves'
wakes.

I wonder what sound
my native basalt makes
as it bubbles
deep in Earth's volcanic throat,
bakes, broils and rises to
a black crust?

Suddenly I know.
It's sad and low.

Sad as sea-spray on the Causeway is exuberant.
Aeons flown,
of snowflakes blown
in high-note water tones.
It has almost forgot
the slowing of the lava flow.

Daily it feels the tide
plash and pool.

Natural order.
The heart grows cold,
platelets
harden and break.
Its heat congealed,
it stops
as all hearts must.

Section Three
Appendix

Tryst & The Long Wave: were inspired by Druridge Bay and Newbiggin, Northumberland. My love of the sea has been a constant throughout life. I love the British Coastline.

Ships: An Ekphrastic poem after "Ships" by Crystalwizard, original artwork in Bewildering Stories e-zine Issue 272.

Holy Island Haibun & A Song of Seals: The Holy Island of Lindisfarne is off the Northumberland coast and can be reached via a causeway road only twice a day at low tide.

As I Remember It: Portrush, Co Antrim, N Ireland, where I spent many happy childhood hours and most of my student days.

Heart of Stone: Inspired by the Lithophone – Ruskin's Rocks (an instrument made of Cumbrian stone) at Brantwood. You can hear this played by Dame Evelyn Glennie here: vimeo.com/14766100.

Winter-street-with-bench-and-lamp-post-wallpaper
(www.pickywallpapers.com/1366x768/nature/winter/)

Oonah V Joslin

Section Four

The Vow of Silence

It has come to my attention,
said the Abbot to the monks,
that certain of the order
are frequently quite drunk.
I speak of beer and claret.
I speak of mead and must.
I hear of meats and roasts and fish
such foods that grace the daily dish,
leading to gluttony and lust!
And many dishes are contrived,
with spices meant to please the palate;
foods that titillate and delight,
unsanctioned by the rule of prelate
are here prepared by skilful cooks
who study tempting recipes
in place of reading holy books.

At mealtimes the observance
of silent contemplation
is often undermined I'm told
by wild gesticulation
such as is more befitting
to jesters and court players
a silent pandemonium,
of covert conversations
used not as last resort
but for jokes and to report
tales of sexual incontinence;

licentious anecdotes.
Of lewd and unfit behaviour
there is much in evidence!

Some evil festers in this abbey,
said the abbot with a smile;
a lexicon of depravity.
I will linger here a while.

The Smith's Gold

He stoked his pipe and stoked his forge.
Both burned all day in the dark smithy.
His sleeves rolled,
strands of his meagre hair sweat-pasted to his pate,
he breathed the smell
of smoke and iron.

The anvil like a rhino's horn
was a hard place
for bending bars made pliable by fire.
Stooped between hammer and orange flame
his boiler suit sooted, he lived
a life of metal and stone.

He made railings for a rich man's grave.
Took pride in the hot-hearted forge,
words of sacred wisdom,
the broad band he wore,
the only gold he'd ever want or know.

Sparks flew as his sinuous arm drew
down each hammer blow
and every spark rang free
as his spirit
fired up,
hammered down;
he died before his time.

Forge ahead.
Burn, burn like an evening sun.
Always the final stroke was his.

A Perception of Demeter

Autumn's rainbow should burnish the sky in sudden violet pewter and bright steel, darkly tarnished sliver, yellow brass, bronze and every cast of copper. Gold-laden bough to berry; gong of Sun's demise, harvest-pale moonrise streaks November's sleet: a metallic spectrum to reflect the forge of Winter burning to bare ash.

Advent

I light a candle.
There's no need
except a desire for flickering
warmth and dancing fire.

I light a candle;
watch the primal
space that is infra-red,
with scientific detachment.

My candle is not tallow
spermaceti or beeswax
but a hydrocarbon
by-product of ocean-bed

long dead; not very romantic,
not very devotional.
I will mark off
feast days in candle hours

invest festive emotion
into each illumination;
invoke times past
and eke the darks days out

with thoughts of
loved ones gone
and loved ones far
and near. Year on year

I light a candle.
There's no need
except the heart's deep yearning
for some ancestral hearth.

Dream of a Frost Sprite

The frost sprite grasped the lamppost and danced. Around she spun, snow clothing her form so her ice-dress sparkled like candy-floss. Flurries whisked her from tree to lamppost, partner to a million snowflakes until she lay exhausted on a drift. Asleep in a deep blanket, she dreamt of her lover.

Oonah V Joslin

Change Has Tenses All Its Own

The Present Continuous
now and now and now
that goes unnoticed in the sweep of days
is seldom spoken of in conversation,
wreaks its havoc little by little
in subtle,
cumulative ways.

The Future Fast Historic
alters everything in one
life changing,
heart pounding,
significant moment of
such clarity that
the light of its revelation shocks us:
stops us in the now.

The Future Perfect where,
unaware,
we will have been
whatever
it is
we were.

Winter's Last Breath

Blow me a blow of wind high in the tops.
Leafless, still leafless, lifeless winter drops
whiter than bone and through hard bitten ground
delicate bells push up and make no sound.
Screech me a screech would make a spirit quake.
Moan all around, leave terror in your wake.
Frighten mere children while it's in your power.
This is your final battle, your last hour.
Yes, you have fight but you can't win the day.
Change as change happens. Spring is on her way.
Look, I have taken off my winter vest.
See how gently light rain comes to rest
there on your grave, old withered winter wind.
Sleep there a while until the season's turned.
Go now, let bird song tune you from my mind.

A Cemetery Just Around the Corner

The dead cast long shadows
on January ground.
Foreshortened cremations rest
like pillows on their graves.

A recent burial
hummocked among hollows,
blanketed still in white flowers
deep as a duvet,
deep as snow,
dares to supersede
older depressions.

Here lie the long dead
in a hare's scrape
under collapsed mole hills.
In the corner there,
broken and weathered,
markers crumble
as if they'd never been.

My footfall makes no sound.
My presence goes unseen.

Stain of Light

Shattered shards of fractured light that I am,
I illuminated sacred text, shone
on the faces of the congregation,
presented Christ arisen to the world,
fragile and invincible, set aloft,
a witness, a light to lighten gentiles,
the pride of Christendom. I held the sun
close in my leaden heart; the Son, Kýrie eléison.

There is no mercy in time's sacrilege.
Centuries ground to fusty pews,
degraded mortar, silent hymns, prayers
all forgotten, past.

Lord have mercy on this relic of glass
only begotten of the minds of men
and fashioned by faith.

Section 4
Appendix

Vow of Silence: When Gerald of Wales (c1146 - c1223) visited Canterbury he apparently found the brothers had developed sign language which circumvented the vow of silence and was being used to more sophisticated ends than, 'Please pass the salt.'

Dream of a Frost Sprite: was inspired by Winter Street with Bench and Lamp Post.

Stains of light on the floor of Lincoln Cathedral Feb 2015 – Oonah V Joslin

Section Five

Phase Transition

In the phase transition
body to soul
all energy recycled
freed from the fermion flow
that makes this universe
tick

outside of time
inside the mind of god
I will be
like a fish that
knows water is wet
a bird that needs
no air for flight.

They may take out my brain
put it in a jar.
'There,' they will say,
'that was her brain.'

Voluntary Exile

I flee to Lothlórien when I feel low,
dive between those ever-fresh white sheets,
commune with elves on paper primrose paths
under innocent skies and yellow sun
where kindness and imagination meet and dance
to silence, as when Earth was young.

Or in the forest glade under the clear blue,
I meet fawns on the Dancing Lawn,
talk with true Narnians and water sprites,
watch the trees eat chocolate-mousse soil —
the waters bubble up brown, frothy draughts.
I hope for a glimpse of Aslan or Gandalf.

There all I love is perfectly described.
Elegant cadences have survived the mangling
of the spoken word. The sword is always just.
The blade cannot be bought. Laughter
is a gift much sought after. Money,
for its own sake, has no meaning

as in the 24th century,
on a planet far away, Trekking
some distant quadrant of the galaxy.
Under a pink sky and purple seas
Captain Benevolent puts alien species at their ease.
No one 'gets evicted'. Prime Directive. Please,

what dishonesty.
I close the book,
stop the film,
try to switch off, escape
along a beach,
allow the grains to sandblast my thoughts clean,

yet conscious always of the politics
of the sea, the never-ending ebb
of history, my little place in its maelstrom.
Quiet on the margin of the tide,
at the centre of my self-made storm,
still I feel the sunshine of Lothlórien.

Art of the Storm

Against the Olympian sky of the great storm
interlaced rings bright
winking
eye to the weather
we watched kittiwakes nest
a narrow ledge on the Baltic Mill
lulled by the natural music of the flow
relayed upwards
amplified.

From the Sage, green
contoured clouds cascaded
rocked to the crack
burst new bolts to the Tyne Bridge
with fiery finger
relayed downwards
amplified.

Walls and walls endless
constant grey and horizontal
rain hid the city all from view
roads gushed rivers
no through traffic
relayed chaos
amplified.

And had we seen that mushrooming
of cloud that settled on the city
from above
witnessed that extreme
fear might have stormed our hearts
amplified.

I feared for the kittiwakes.

Music to my Ears

I'm not a Stradivarius
my pitch is too precarious,
my understanding of crochets and quavers
wavers.
I'm not mellow like a cello
or bright like Steinway high notes – more yellow.
I don't project, I bellow
like a crumhorn; not high octave sound
but kind of contralto bassoonahish, round
of body -- an ill tempered clavier missing a note.
I should let the frog in my throat
do the singing,
the talking,
find the harmonica
for the gin and the tonica.
My dijeridoo doesn't.
My kazoo wasn't.
My accordion lacks accord. Heated discussion
drowns out my arrhythmic percussion.
Silence is the best music I have ever heard;
that or the song of a single springtime bird.

Notes on Loss

Birds greet sunrise as
they have always done. But I
hear fewer high notes.
Every spring has older ears;
little sense of renewal.

Touching the Tiger

Tantalising, close it lies.

Would you like to touch the tiger skin?
asks the man in the pith helmet.
Every tiger is unique.
You know them by their stripes
a different pattern every one
remarkable.

Shaken loose
there its ears
and eyeholes.

I drop
the thing.

Lost
its living gold and roar

patterns
torn asunder
darkness
dread and threat
declawed

discarded drape of a tattered tiger.

No breath.
No tiger breath.

No rippling gold.
No bold feline predator.
Behold

the fearful
asymmetry of death.

Seeing – Through the Wardrobe Door
(for C S Lewis)

He lived in shadow lands
where this world is a crack
in the paving of heaven;
all hell, a stretched privation of the soul.

He consorted with planetary
angels but he knew demons too
and that stars are more
than what they are made of.

He was alchemic in his language,
loud of speech, intemperate of tone.
But to him we all were Hnau;
blood of his blood; bone of his bone;

partakers of life in the flesh;
needing both the light
and what the light shows
to transcend.

All That There Is

Everywhere at once the wave breaks on a shore
unknowable. Not created. Not destroyed. It moves
through mediums dark, unseen on some immeasurable
scale alien to linear time.

One infinite moment collapses dark energy on a ledge of
liminality and there is Light; a frothy bubble on the
forward tide of the four percent we think we know.

Son et Lumière.
All that there is. A Moment.
Bang and Starburst.

Transference our progenitor, matter our flesh: we are the
measure of this great release and trailing waves of energy
we come, crashing into consciousness: wonder for a brief
expanse what forces move and whence they came.

We break once more on the unknown; give back our
energy; emerge we know not where; perhaps at the
beginning.

Same Place as the Music
(for cinematographer Andrew Lesnie)

Three pounds of cells
in a dark bone box
play out the action

subjectively

interpreting,
communicating
every perception

sound, sense and light

that colour the momentary
ever-changing
synaptic self.

Who calls the shots?

We've barely seen behind the lens.
barely grasped where the light comes from;
same place as the music

perhaps. And at the end

darkness and silence may hold wonder
without this grey mass
in which we learn the rapture of living
happily ever after.

I want the light
and music to be
real.

Section 5
Appendix

Art of the Storm: The Baltic Centre for Contemporary Art is situated on the south bank of the River Tyne, Gateshead/Newcastle upon Tyne. This poem refers to the super-cell storm of 28th June 2012.
The Sage Gateshead is a concert venue and also a centre for musical education, located in Gateshead on the south bank of the River Tyne.

Seeing – Through the Wardrobe Door: From Meditation in a Tool Shed – C S Lewis 'The people who look at things have had it all their own way; the people who look along things have simply been brow-beaten. It has even come to be taken for granted that the external account of a thing somehow refutes or "debunks" the account given from inside. "All these moral ideals which look so transcendental and beautiful from inside," says the wiseacre, "are really only a mass of biological instincts and inherited taboos." And no one plays the game the other way round by replying, "If you will only step inside, the things that look to you like instincts and taboos will suddenly reveal their real and transcendental nature." Lewis later used this idea to describe the dwarves, who in "The Last Battle" were altogether unable to experience bliss because of the darkness within them. Hnau in Lewis' book "Out of the Silent Planet" embodies the concept of Beings having an intrinsic value.

All That There Is: Aged 12, I discovered this passage from Wordsworth which has always remained with me, hence, "trailing waves of energy we come,"
Ode 536 Intimations of Immortality.

"Our birth is but a sleep and a forgetting:

The Soul that rises with us, our life's Star,
    Hath had elsewhere its setting,

And cometh from afar:
Not in entire forgetfulness,
And not in utter nakedness,
But trailing clouds of glory do we come
From God, who is our home:"

Same Place as the Music: Actor Sean Astin to the late Andrew Lesnie, (Cinematographer of The Lord of the Rings):
"Where is the light coming from?"
[...] At this moment there was light in a scene where there would have been no source for it.
"He looked at me and he just said 'Same place as the music.'"

Bio

Oonah Yvonne Joslin (nee Kyle) was born in Ballymena, Co Antrim in 1954. Her first love was poetry and telling stories. Early poems were published in Ballymena Academy's magazine. In 2006 she resigned from teaching, joined writewords.org.uk and became addicted to flash. To her astonishment she won three Microhorror prizes. Oonah's stories and poems have been published in various print anthologies. The first part of her novella 'A Genie in a Jam', is serialised at 'Bewildering Stories'. She was managing editor at Every Day Poets for 5 years after which she became poetry editor at The Linnet's Wings.

You can follow Oonah on Facebook or at her blog Parallel Oonahverse.

PUBLICATIONS

Binnacle Short Poetry Honourable Mention 2009/2011
Diamond Twig Poem poem of the month Apr 2011/July 2012
Micro Horror Prize winner 2007/2008/2009

Print Anthologies:

Short Story U S Library
Static Poetry II, III
Toe Tags 2009
Pangea Writewords Anthology 2012
New Sun Rising Stories for Japan 2012
Another 100 Horrors 2013
The Very Best of Every Day Fiction 1,2 &3
Poems for a Liminal Age 2015
The Sea – Rebel Poetry 2015
Twisted Tales 2012/2013/2016
Be Not Afraid: An Anthology in Appreciation of Seamus Heaney 2016

Magzines and E-Zines
A New Ulster, Apollo's Lyre
Backhand Stories, Bewildering Stories, Blink Ink, Boston Literary Review
Clockwise Cat
Demon Minds, Doorknobs and Bodypaint
Every Day Fiction
Flash Fiction Chronicles, Flashes in the Dark, Flashquake
Gyroscope Review
Ink Sweat & Tears
Left Hand Waving
MicroHorror, Modicum
Ofi Press, Open Mouse
Postcard Poems and Prose, Postcard Shorts
Short Fiction UK, Short Humour, Static Movement
The Linnet's Wings, The Pygmy Giant, The Ranfurly Review, The Shine Journal
and Joyful, The View from Here, Tweetthemeat
Victorian Violet Press
Zoomorphic Poetry part 2
5 x 5 Fiction, 5 minute fiction, 10Flash